AT THE SEASIDE

Illustrations by Angela Mitson Written by Giles Reed

First published 1979 in Great Britain by
Studio Publications (Ipswich) Ltd.,
32, Princes Street, Ipswich, England.

Colour origination by Colour Craftsmen Ltd, Silver End, Essex.
Printed and bound by Sackville Press Billericay Ltd, Billericay, Essex.

Limp Edition : ISBN 0 904584 78 X
Hard Back Edition : ISBN 0 904584 56 9

The Sun was shining very brightly.
It was a very hot day, and all the Munch Bunch felt very lazy.

Suddenly, Spud jumped to his feet.
"Let's all go to the seaside," he shouted.
"What a great idea," said Pedro Orange.
And all the Munch Bunch agreed with him.

They collected their buckets and spades from Professor Peabody ...... and their swimsuits from their own homes. Very soon, they were ready for their big day out.

They all climbed into Spud's car and trailer ... and off they went to the seaside.
All except Olly Onion that is – he preferred to go on his bike.

They soon arrived at the beach.
Emma Apple, Lizzie Leek and Olive went for a swim...
Olly Onion was fishing...
And Pippa Pear and Adam Avocado went for a picnic – to eat!

Pedro Orange had fallen asleep in his deck chair — until Suzie Celery "accidently" tipped water over him.
Naughty Suzie was up to her tricks again.

Suddenly there was a loud shriek from one of the Munch Bunch.
It was Olly Onion.
A crab had bitten his toe.
And he had lost his fishing rod in the water.
Poor Olly!

"Don't worry," said Tom Tomato, "we'll get it back for you." So Tom, Spud and Scruff dived in to rescue Olly's rod.

Meanwhile, Supercool was having a great time.
He had made himself a surf board and was whizzing over the water.
Very Fast.

Casper Carrot thought that surfing looked too dangerous.
So he went rowing in a little boat with Spud and Corny - on-the-cob.

Peabody was busy too.
He had brought his metal detector
with him and was looking for
valuable coins.

And Pippa Pear and Adam Avocado?
They were still eating!

Spud thought it was about time they did something different.
So he organised a sand-castle competition.
Lucy Lemon was making a special sand-castle with a moat.
So Tom went to get some water for her in his bucket.

Tom is always happy when he is helping someone...

But he always does it wrong.
Poor Tom.
He didn't know that all the water had fallen out of the holes in his bucket.
And Lucy didn't have the heart to tell him.

But......further along the beach Suzie stood with Scruff and Billy.
And they had very naughty looks in their eyes.

Suddenly, DISASTER.
Scruff Gooseberry and his friends Billy Blackberry and Suzie Celery jumped right on the sand-castles. They knocked them all down.

What a naughty thing to do.

Spud had to think again.
Quickly.
He thought that a game of football would keep them out of mischief.

But Wally Walnut kicked the ball into the sea.
And that was the end of that!

Professor Peabody, meanwhile, had made a Punch and Judy show.
And everybody was happy.
Except poor Olive.
Because she was so small she could not see anything at all..

Until Spud picked her up and put her on his shoulders.

Emma Apple is a very vain apple. She was determined to get a nice sun tan to make her look prettier. But as the day wore on, all she got was redder and redder and redder. Silly Emma!

It was almost time for the beach party.
Lizzie Leek and Button Mushroom were busy preparing the sausages.
And who else do you think wanted to help with the food?
Yes — Pippa Pear!

The Munch Bunch enjoyed the beach party very much. There was singing and dancing and eating and drinking and swimming and.....
Well, everyone did just what they wanted to do.

And when they went home that night, they all agreed that it had been a really super day.

Other MUNCH BUNCH Books available

IN THIS SERIES

MEET THE MUNCH BUNCH
THE MUNCH BUNCH AT THE SEASIDE
THE MUNCH BUNCH GO CAMPING
THE MUNCH BUNCH HAVE A PARTY

ALSO AVAILABLE

SPUD
OLLY ONION
PETE PEPPER
LIZZIE LEEK
BILLY BLACKBERRY
BOUNCE
PROFESSOR PEABODY
SUPERCOOL
SALLY STRAWBERRY
TOM TOMATO
BUTTON AND TINY
THE BANANA BUNCH

AVAILABLE SOON

PIPPA PEAR
PEANUT
WALLY WALNUT
ADAM AVOCADO
PEDRO ORANGE
EMMA APPLE
LUCY LEMON
OLIVE
CORNY-ON-THE-COB
CASPER CARROT
SCRUFF GOOSEBERRY
SUZIE CELERY

Super MUNCH BUNCH Offer

POSTER... size $17\frac{1}{2}'' \times 24\frac{1}{2}''$ of all the MUNCH BUNCH.
Printed in full colour on high quality paper and laminated to keep it clean.
Send £1 cheque or postal order made payable to Studio Publications (Ipswich) Ltd, to:

Studio Publications (Ipswich) Ltd.,
32, Princes Street,
Ipswich. IP1 1RJ.

Please state your name and address clearly
Price includes post and packing.
Offer valid to December 1980.